UNIVERSITY OF
OREGON DUCKS®
COOKBOOK

C. J. GIFFORD

PHOTOGRAPHS BY ZAC WILLIAMS

GIBBS SMITH
TO ENRICH AND INSPIRE HUMANKIND

First Edition
16 15 14 13 12   5 4 3 2 1

Published by
Gibbs Smith
P.O. Box 667
Layton, Utah 84041

1.800.835.4993 orders
www.gibbs-smith.com

Printed and bound in China

Gibbs Smith books are printed on either recycled, 100% post-consumer
waste, FSC-certified papers or on paper produced from sustainable PEFC-
certified forest/controlled wood source. Learn more at www.pefc.org.

Library of Congress Cataloging-in-Publication Data

Gifford, C. J.
University of Oregon Ducks cookbook / C. J. Gifford ;
photographs by Zac Williams.
p. cm.
ISBN 978-1-4236-3006-7
1. Outdoor cooking. 2. Oregon Ducks (Football team) 3. Cooking—
Oregon. 4. Tailgate parties—Oregon—Eugene. 5. Football fans—Oregon—
Eugene. 6. University of Oregon—Football—Miscellanea.
I. Title.
TX823.G493 2012
642'.309795—dc23
2012011730

CONTENTS

O-Zone
CHICKEN DIP

Ingredients

2 boneless, skinless chicken
   breasts, cooked

1 1/2 cups Lights Out
   Sauce (recipe follows)

1 package (8 ounces)
   cream cheese, softened

1 cup bleu cheese dressing

2 cups grated cheddar cheese

✳ Serves 10–12 ✳

Preheat oven to 325 degrees. Cut chicken into small pieces or shred it and mix with Lights Out Sauce in a medium bowl; set aside.

Spread the cream cheese on the bottom of a 7 x 11-inch baking dish and evenly distribute chicken mixture on top. Pour dressing over chicken and cover with cheddar cheese.

Bake for 35 minutes or until cheese bubbles. Serve with sliced bread or crackers.

The O-Zone is potentially damaging in Eugene, to visiting teams that is.

Lights Out Sauce

³/₄ cup bottled red-hot or cayenne pepper sauce

¹/₂ cup cold butter, cut into cubes

¹/₄ cup packed light brown sugar

1 tablespoon minced garlic

1 tablespoon Worcestershire sauce

Cracked black pepper, to taste

Carefully pour hot sauce into a small saucepan and add butter, making sure cubes are separated. Turn on heat to low and add brown sugar, garlic, and Worcestershire sauce; stirring constantly until mixture simmers.

When sauce reaches a low boil, cook for 2 minutes, stirring continuously. Remove from heat and let cool for 30 minutes until sauce thickens.

5

Bowl Bound
SALSA

Ingredients

5 ripe red tomatoes (not Roma)

Kosher or coarse sea salt, to taste

$1/2$ cup fresh cilantro leaves, finely chopped

4 large cloves garlic, finely chopped

1 small onion, finely chopped

1 small jalapeno, finely chopped

1 small lime, juiced

Cracked black pepper, to taste

✳ Serves 10–12 ✳

Dice tomatoes and place into a large bowl; sprinkle with a pinch of salt. Add cilantro, garlic, onion, and jalapeno and gently mix—avoid juicing tomatoes. Pour off any liquid so the salsa is moist, but not watery. Sprinkle lime juice over salsa and mix well. Refrigerate 1 hour before serving.

Add additional salt and pepper, to taste, and serve with chips. For a cute serving idea, line a ball cap or helmet with napkins and fill with chips.

The Ducks first went to the Rose Bowl in 1917. Both the Ducks and the salsa are looking to get into another bowl soon.

Quackers
AND CHEESE

Ingredients

1 pound sliced medium cheddar cheese, cold

Duck-shaped metal cookie cutter

Crackers or baked chips, of choice

✳ Serves 8–10 ✳

Place cheese slices on a hard surface covered with a piece of parchment paper. Press duck-shaped cutter firmly into each cheese slice. The duck shapes will drop out with light pressure when kept cold. Arrange on a tray with your favorite crackers.

More than 30 types of ducks make their home in the U.S., but only one type matters to Oregonians.

Autzen NACHOS

Ingredients

5 chicken breast tenders

1/4 teaspoon chili powder

1/4 teaspoon diced onion

2 cups water, divided

1 small lime, juiced, divided

1 bag (15 ounces)
tortilla chips

8 ounces grated
cheddar cheese

8 ounces grated Mexican-
blend cheese

1 small purple onion,
sliced into thin strips

1 can (15 ounces) black
beans, rinsed, drained,
and warmed

1 can (4.2 ounces) sliced
black olives, drained

1 small jalapeno,
sliced into rings

✳ Serves 8–10 ✳

Preheat oven to 375 degrees. Place chicken in medium saucepan and add chili powder, diced onion, 1 cup water, and 1/2 tablespoon lime juice; cover and heat on high until liquid is gone.

Just as chicken begins to brown in the hot, dry pan, remove from heat, transfer to a cutting board, and cut or shred into small pieces. Return chicken to hot pan and carefully add 1/2 cup water. Turn chicken so it's well covered and turns a reddish-brown color. Add remaining water and remove from heat. Set aside.

Cover the bottom of a large baking sheet with a layer of chips. Sprinkle some lime juice lightly over chips and then sprinkle with a layer of the combined cheeses. Add one-third of the onion and spoon beans on top. Add olives, reserving a few for the last layer.

Add another layer of chips, a sprinkle of lime juice, cheeses, onion, and top with chicken. Add remaining chips, cheeses, and onion. Scatter jalapeno and olive slices over top and bake 5–6 minutes or until cheese melts throughout and bubbles on top.

Autzen Stadium is known to be one of the loudest stadiums in the country with an official capacity of only 54,000.

11

Eugene
HIPPY DIP

Ingredients

1 jar (6.5 ounces) marinated
  artichoke hearts

$1/2$ cup mayonnaise

Finely grated
  Parmesan cheese

Pinch of crushed red
  pepper flakes

✳ Serves 4–6 ✳

Preheat oven to 400 degrees.

Drain artichoke hearts, pouring excess oil out of jar and set aside. Slice artichokes into bite-size pieces and place in a medium bowl.

Add mayonnaise to empty jar and fill remaining space with Parmesan cheese and red pepper flakes; stir. Add mix to artichokes and blend well. Transfer dip to a shallow, oven-proof serving dish and wipe excess off sides of dish. Bake 15 minutes or until top browns and bubbles.

Remove excess grease off top before serving with crackers.

Eugene gives a nod to its hippy roots by leading the state in granola consumption, recycling, and tie-dye wardrobes.

Quack Attack™
BRUSCHETTA

Ingredients

2 tablespoons extra
virgin olive oil

4 tablespoons
balsamic vinegar

6 firm, ripe Roma
tomatoes, chopped
into ¼-inch pieces

Kosher or coarse sea
salt, to taste

Cracked black
pepper, to taste

1 large red onion, chopped

10 cloves garlic, finely diced

¼ cup fresh basil
leaves, finely sliced

1 baguette, thinly sliced

Shaved Parmesan cheese
curls, for garnish

✳ Serves 10–12 ✳

Stir oil and vinegar together in a large bowl. Add tomatoes and sprinkle with salt and pepper; let sit for 5 minutes.

Gently stir onion, garlic, and basil into tomatoes; mix well. Add more vinegar or pepper, to taste. Serve immediately or cover and refrigerate until serving.

Serve by spooning onto baguette slices and topping with Parmesan curls.

Like many birds, ducks can be docile creatures. Oregon Ducks® are not, especially when they're on Quack Attack.™

Hail Oregon®
CAESAR

Ingredients

1 large lemon

3 large cloves garlic, minced

Extra virgin olive oil

1 cup grated Parmesan cheese

Cracked black pepper, to taste

1 large head romaine lettuce, torn into bite-size pieces

Croutons

✳ Serves 4–6 ✳

Juice lemon into lidded jar. Remove any seeds. Add garlic. Matching the amount of juice and garlic in the bottom of the jar, carefully pour in an equal amount of oil. Add cheese and black pepper to mixture. Cover jar and let stand 15 minutes. Shake well before pouring over lettuce in a large bowl. Toss salad with dressing, add croutons, and more pepper, if desired.

Like Julius Caesar, the Oregon Ducks® have many competitors, most notably the Oregon State Beavers.

Oregon® Goal
SLAW

Ingredients

1/3 cup mayonnaise

2 tablespoons sugar

1 tablespoon cider vinegar

1 tablespoon plain
   Greek yogurt

Dash lemon juice

1 bag (14 ounces) carrot
   and cabbage slaw mix

1/4 teaspoon caraway seeds

Cracked black
   pepper, to taste

* Serves 4–6 *

Whip mayonnaise, sugar, vinegar, yogurt, and lemon juice together in a large bowl until well blended.

Add slaw mix and caraway seeds; stir until slaw is coated. Refrigerate for 1 hour. Stir before serving and add pepper, to taste.

There are goal lines, goal posts, blocked goals, and field goals and everyone in the Oregon Ducks® football program sets their goals high.

I Love My
DUCK WINGS

Ingredients

12 chicken party wings

1 tablespoon chili powder

$1/2$ teaspoon cayenne pepper

$1/4$ teaspoon dry mustard

$1/4$ teaspoon turmeric

Dash cumin, optional

**$1/4$ teaspoon kosher
or coarse sea salt**

**$1/4$ tablespoon cracked
black pepper**

1 tablespoon minced garlic

**2 tablespoons extra
virgin olive oil**

2 tablespoons cider vinegar

* Serves 6–10 *

Wash and dry wings and set aside in a large bowl.

In a small bowl, combine dry ingredients and then stir in garlic, oil, and vinegar. Pour sauce over wings and turn to coat. Refrigerate for 30 minutes.

Preheat oven to 375 degrees and line a baking sheet with parchment paper.

Place wings on baking sheet in a single layer. Spoon additional sauce over wings and bake for 30 minutes. Remove from oven, turn wings over, and bake another 10 minutes or until crunchy.

In 2009, Supwitchugirl's YouTube video, *I Love My Ducks*, became an instant anthem as the Oregon Ducks® raced to the Rose Bowl.

Webfoot
SPEC-TATERS

Ingredients

6 small baking
    potatoes, baked

2 tablespoons extra
    virgin olive oil

Kosher or coarse sea
    salt, to taste

Cracked black
    pepper, to taste

2 cloves garlic, finely minced

1 bag (8 ounces) grated
    cheddar cheese

1/3 cup crumbled bacon

2 green onions, white parts
    cut into 1/4-inch pieces
    and greens thinly sliced

1 pint sour cream or
    Greek yogurt

* Serves 12 *

Preheat oven to 350 degrees and line a baking sheet with parchment paper.

Cut potatoes in half lengthwise. Scoop out the flesh of each potato half with a spoon, leaving about a 1/4-inch thick wall. Lightly brush the insides of the potato skins with oil and place, cut side up, on prepared baking sheet. Sprinkle potatoes with salt and pepper and add a small amount of garlic to each half. Bake for 8 minutes.

Remove from oven and quickly add 1 tablespoon, or more to taste, of cheese to each potato. Evenly divide bacon among potato halves and place under broiler until cheese melts and browns. Remove from oven and place on a serving platter. Top with onion pieces, a dollop of sour cream, and a sprinkling of onion greens.

Before they were Ducks, they were Webfoots, and while the university formally dropped the funky foot reference in the early 1900s, it resurfaced in the 60s and remains an accepted adjective for fans.

End Zone
ROASTED GARLIC

Ingredients

2 cups cloves garlic, peeled and ends trimmed

$1^{1}/_{4}$ teaspoons extra virgin olive oil

$^{1}/_{4}$ teaspoon kosher or coarse sea salt

$^{1}/_{4}$ teaspoon cracked black pepper

✻ Serves 8 ✻

Preheat oven to 400 degrees.

Combine all ingredients in a small microwave-safe bowl until cloves are fully coated in oil. Microwave on high for 2 minutes. Spread cloves into a shallow, oven-proof serving dish and bake for 8 minutes or until tops are brown. Spread on sliced bread or crackers.

While it's a thrill to earn points in the end zone, excessive celebrating results in a 15-yard penalty. However, up in the Autzen stands, post-point celebrating is often excessive and accepted.

Emerald City
SALAD

Ingredients

5 cups chopped broccoli

1 yellow bell pepper, cut
   into $1/2$-inch pieces

$1/4$ cup diced white onion

$1/2$ cup mayonnaise

$1/4$ cup sugar

1 tablespoon rice vinegar

1 tablespoon white vinegar

$1/4$ cup crumbled bacon

$1/4$ cup sunflower seeds

1 cup diced Swiss cheese

* Serves 6–8 *

Combine broccoli, bell pepper, and onion in a large bowl.

In a small bowl, stir mayonnaise and sugar together and then add vinegars. Stir well and pour over vegetables; thoroughly combine. Chill for 30 minutes.

Add bacon, sunflower seeds, and cheese before serving.

Sure, Dorothy got lost in it and our neighbors to the north like to coin it for Seattle, but Eugene is Oregon's Emerald City.

Deviled
DUCK EGGS

Ingredients

8 eggs, hard-boiled,
  cooked, and peeled

$1/4$ cup mayonnaise

2 teaspoons prepared
  mustard

$1/4$ teaspoon dill relish

Pinch of salt

Paprika

2 tablespoons
  chopped chives

✳ Serves 12–16 ✳

Slice eggs in half, remove yolks, and set aside.

Add yolks to a medium bowl with mayonnaise, mustard, relish, and salt and mix well.

Arrange egg whites on a serving tray and spoon yolk mixture decoratively into each egg. Sprinkle lightly with paprika and chives.

Most duck eggs take 26–30 days to hatch, but you can make this in less than an hour.

Civil War
SLICES

Ingredients

2 green onions, white parts cut into 1/4-inch pieces and greens sliced on an angle

1 tablespoon extra virgin olive oil

1 tablespoon minced garlic

1/4 teaspoon cracked black pepper

1/4 teaspoon paprika

1/4 teaspoon celery salt

1/4 teaspoon marjoram or thyme

1/2 teaspoon kosher or coarse sea salt

5 medium-large baking potatoes, cut into wedges

1 container (5.3 ounces) non-fat Greek yogurt

1 small carrot, coarsely grated

Preheat oven to 450 degrees.

Place white onion pieces in a large bowl and combine with oil and spices. Add potatoes and coat well by stirring with a spatula.

Place wedges skin side down on a baking sheet. Cover with any remaining spices and oil and bake for 15 minutes. Remove from oven, turn over potatoes, and bake another 15 minutes or until edges of wedges are crispy.

Place yogurt in a serving bowl, add carrot on top, and cover with green onion slices. Serve with potatoes.

Green always covers orange. The Oregon Civil War is the 7th oldest rivalry in U.S. college football, pitting the green and yellow U of O Ducks® against the orange and black OSU Beavers®.

✳ Serves 6 ✳

Hurried–Huddle FISH TACOS

Ingredients

4 frozen white fish filets
in plastic pouches

1 medium red onion,
thinly sliced

1 teaspoon extra
virgin olive oil

3 cloves garlic, thinly sliced

1 cup chicken broth

1 small lime, juiced

5 ounces non-fat plain
Greek yogurt

2 cloves garlic, minced

Small sprig cilantro, chopped

Cracked black
pepper, to taste

Kosher or coarse sea
salt, optional

1 bag (14 ounces) carrot
and cabbage slaw mix

8 tortillas

✳ Serves 8 ✳

Place frozen filets in pouches in a large bowl. Cover completely with cold water and let sit for 20 minutes or until fish is partially thawed and firm.

Heat a large skillet to medium high and cook onion in oil for 5 minutes or until lightly browned. Remove filets from plastic and lay on top of onion. Add sliced garlic to top of fish. When the oil is very hot and the skillet is almost dry, slowly add half of the broth and flip filets.

As pan dries a second time, slowly add remaining broth and half the lime juice. Reduce heat and cover; cooking for about 5 minutes. Fish is done when it easily flakes with a fork.

Mix yogurt, minced garlic, remaining lime juice, cilantro, and pepper in a serving bowl. Season with a pinch of salt, if desired.

To serve, place a handful of slaw mix on a tortilla and add half of one filet. Top with yogurt sauce.

Eat your dinner standing up and don't blink— Oregon's hurry-up offense often results in no huddle at all. There's a chance they'll score before you've got the first bite in.

Stadium Screamer
STEAMERS

Ingredients

2 pounds small, fresh
   manila clams

$1/2$ cup butter or margarine

1 cup non-alcoholic
   white wine

1 cup chicken broth

1 lemon, juiced

2 tablespoons minced garlic

4 green onions, chopped

$1/2$ teaspoon kosher
   or coarse sea salt

$1/3$ teaspoon cracked
   black pepper

✳ Serves 6–8 ✳

Rinse clams and set aside.

Melt butter in a medium stock pot. Add liquids, garlic, onions, salt, and pepper. Place clams in pot, cover, and bring to a boil. Clams are done when they open, about 5 minutes. Discard any unopened clams.

Ladle clams and broth into bowls and serve with crusty bread.

Autzen's decibel level is so high that other teams often clam up during offensive huddles.

Mighty Oregon®
FLANKER STEAK

Ingredients

- 1/2 teaspoon soy sauce
- 1/4 cup balsamic vinegar
- 2 teaspoons minced garlic
- 1/4 cup minced red onion
- 1 pound beef flat iron or flank steak
- Sideline Sauce (recipe follows)
- Baguette

✱ Serves 6 ✱

Combine soy sauce, vinegar, garlic, and onion in a small bowl and then pour into a large ziplock bag. Place steak inside the bag, press out excess air, and seal. Gently massage steak with the marinade and then refrigerate 30–45 minutes.

Remove meat from refrigerator 20 minutes before grilling. Heat grill to high.

Fully flatten meat on hot grill. Cook 4 minutes on each side. Remove and place on a large cutting board. Let it sit 5 minutes before slicing meat into thin strips.

Serve with Sideline Sauce on thinly sliced baguette.

Sideline Sauce

- 2 teaspoons grated horseradish
- 3 tablespoons mayonnaise

Mix together horseradish and mayonnaise in a small bowl and serve.

Stand up and cheer! Join in singing the Duck's fight song, *Mighty Oregon!*

U of O™
FOOTBOLI

Ingredients

1 loaf frozen bread dough, thawed

3 large mushrooms, thinly sliced

1/4 cup thinly sliced red onion

3 large cloves garlic, thinly sliced

1 can (4.2 ounces) chopped black olives

1/2 teaspoon extra virgin olive oil, more for prep work

1 jar (14 ounces) pizza or spaghetti sauce, divided

1 package (5 ounces) sliced Canadian bacon

1 bag (8 ounces) grated mozzarella cheese, divided

1 package (8 ounces) sliced salami or turkey salami

continued on facing page

Preheat oven to 350 degrees. Place bread dough in an oiled bowl.

Place mushrooms, onion, and garlic into a large bowl. Add olives and olive oil; mix well.

Roll 30 inches of parchment paper out onto a flat surface. Rub a small amount of oil onto the middle of the paper. Lightly oil your hands and place dough on the oiled paper. The dough will easily deflate and become pliable, but be careful not to rip or tear it. Spread dough out into a 12 x 24-inch rectangle, pulling to edges of parchment that is not covered with oil. It will stay in place but crinkle paper. Cut 2 thin 12-inch strips of dough and set aside to make laces and stripes for Footboli.

Spread 2 tablespoons sauce on the short side of dough. Spoon 3/4 cup mushroom mixture onto the sauce and top with 3 slices Canadian bacon. Add 1/2 cup cheese and carefully fold over. Repeat, using a liberal amount of sauce, replacing Canadian bacon with 6 slices of salami and 12 slices of pepperoni. Add cheese and fold over. Repeat salami and pepperoni layer and fold over.

**1 package (4.5 ounces)
sliced pepperoni or
turkey pepperoni**

✳ Makes 2 Footboli,
about 12 servings ✳

Now at the half-way point of the dough, cut dough in half with a sharp knife and separate dough pieces. Tuck ends of dough under the roll and gently shape into a football oval. Cut parchment with scissors and lift Footboli and parchment onto a baking sheet. Add dough laces and stripes, tucking gently into the top so they don't curl while baking. Bake 35 minutes or until top is golden brown. Let cool 10 minutes before slicing and serving.

Repeat process on other half of dough.

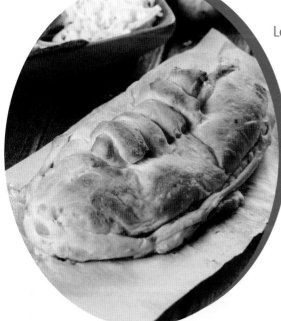

Leather footballs hit the field in 1872. U of O™ Footboli won't last 18 minutes with a crowd of hungry tailgaters.

The Pick
PIGSKIN SLIDERS

Ingredients

**3 pounds boneless
pork butt**

$1/2$ cup packed brown sugar

$1/4$ teaspoon paprika

$1/4$ teaspoon cayenne pepper

**$1/4$ teaspoon cracked
black pepper**

2 teaspoons minced garlic

2 cups apple juice, divided

1 cup barbecue sauce

24 mini slider buns

✻ Serves 24 ✻

Remove visible, excessive fat from pork and discard. Preheat a slow cooker to high.

In a large bowl, stir brown sugar, paprika, and peppers together until well blended. Stir in garlic with a fork, avoiding clumps. Roll pork in mixture until fully covered.

Place pork in prepared slow cooker and add $1 1/2$ cups apple juice; cover. Cook on high for 3 hours. Turn pork and add remaining $1/2$ cup apple juice, cover, and cook another 4–6 hours on medium. (If unable to attend slow cooker for a full 8 hours, add 2 cups of apple juice in beginning.)

Refrigerate cooker until pork fat solidifies. Scrape fat off and discard. Pour liquid out and discard. Using 2 forks, pull meat in opposite directions until well shredded. Add barbecue sauce and mix well; reheat in cooker. When fully reheated, serve on toasted mini slider buns.

The Duck defensive line regularly picks the offense by snatching the opposing ball out of the air then taking it downfield for six. Fans are hungry for more. Luckily, there are plenty of The Pick Pigskin Sliders to go around.

Mo-Center
GRIDIRON BITES

Ingredients

1 cup finely grated
   cheddar cheese

1 green onion, finely diced

$1/4$ cup mayonnaise

$1/4$ cup ketchup

$1/4$ cup prepared mustard

$1/4$ cup dill relish

1 pound ground beef

Cracked black
   pepper, to taste

Barbecue seasoning, to taste

6 mini slider buns

✳ Serves 6 ✳

Mix cheese, onion, ketchup, mustard, and relish in a small bowl.

Pack some ground beef inside a $1/3$ cup measuring cup. Scoop a small hole in the middle of the beef with a 1 tablespoon measuring spoon. Add $1/2$ tablespoon of cheese mixture into the hole and cover with additional beef, firmly packing. Be careful not to squeeze any filling out of the sides of the burgers as they will flare up on grill.

Using a knife, remove burger from cup. Pinch sides if any filling is showing, but retain the shape of the burger. Do not flatten. Set aside and repeat until done. Season with pepper and barbecue seasoning.

Heat grill to medium high. Gently place burgers on grill and cook, carefully flipping only once while cooking. Serve on slider buns. Refrigerate any remaining filling and use within 4 days.

The 117,000 square-foot Moshofsky Center is where Duck football players get their practice game on and learn to take a bite out of the competition.

Marching Band
DRUMMETTES

Ingredients

1/4 cup teriyaki sauce

1 teaspoon soy sauce

1/2 teaspoon extra
   virgin olive oil

1 teaspoon orange
   marmalade

1 teaspoon minced garlic

1/4 cup diced red onion

Cracked black
   pepper, to taste

12 chicken legs

✳ Serves 6 ✳

In a small bowl, stir teriyaki sauce, soy sauce, oil, and marmalade until well blended. Pour into a large ziplock bag. Add garlic, onion, and pepper and shake gently until all ingredients are mixed in the bottom of the bag. Add chicken, close bag, and massage marinade onto meat until well covered. Refrigerate 1–2 hours.

Preheat oven to 350 degrees.

Cover a baking sheet that has sides with parchment paper. Place chicken legs in a tight, alternating formation and cover with any excess marinade. Bake for 30 minutes, turn over legs, and bake another 30 minutes. Turn legs over again and bake an additional 15 minutes or until well browned.

Oregon's marching band treats tailgaters to pregame tunes by splitting up and performing in small groups before kickoff throughout the stadium lot.

Willamette
SLAMMIT

Ingredients

1 scoop (2- to 3-inch ball) lime sherbet

1 cup lemon-lime soda,* divided

3/4 cup ginger ale, divided

Canned whipped topping

Green sprinkles

Regular or diet soda will work, but diet soda will make the sherbet crunchy.

✱ Serves 1 ✱

Fold a towel into a square and place on a firm surface. Place a frozen pint glass onto the towel and quickly drop sherbet into the bottom of the glass.

Working quickly so glass remains frosty; carefully pour 1/2 cup lemon-lime soda on top of the sherbet. Pour 1/2 cup ginger ale into the glass. Add remaining lemon-lime soda and top with remaining ginger ale.

Pick the glass up about 2 inches off of the towel and lightly bounce it up and down until the sherbet pops up to the top of the glass. Swirl a dollop of whipped topping into middle of soda foam. Add green sprinkles and serve with a long spoon and straw.

This recipe is easily multiplied so you can serve all of your friends.

Can't pronounce it? Oregon's Willamette River starts southeast of Eugene and runs about 300 miles until it joins the Columbia River at Portland. It's not the Will-uh-met, it's not the Will-a-mettie, it is simply the Willamette, and now you can slammit.

Waddle It Be
MOCKTAIL

Ingredients

4 Margarita-style glasses or wide-brimmed, stemmed glasses

$1/4$ cup kosher or coarse sea salt

1 fresh lime

1 can (6 ounces) frozen limeade

$1/4$ cup orange juice

4 cups crushed ice

✳ Serves 4 ✳

Pour salt into a wide saucer or plate.

Quarter the lime. Cut a slice in the middle of each wedge, up to the rind. Position one wedge onto each glass at the slice and lightly squeeze it around the rim, moistening it without losing any juice. Remove the limes and set aside for garnishing the glasses.

Dip glasses into salt until rims are covered.

Place limeade, orange juice, and ice into a large blender and mix until slushy. Pour into each glass and garnish with lime wedge, if desired.

Oregon Ducks® run, dive, and fly, but leave waddling to the birds.

UO™
YOO-HOO

Ingredients

2 tablespoons
   chocolate syrup

1 cup cold milk

1/4 teaspoon cinnamon

Canned whipped topping

Green and yellow sprinkles

✳ Serves 1 ✳

Cold Yoo-Hoo

Place chocolate syrup in the bottom of an 8-ounce glass. Pour half of the milk in, stir, and add cinnamon. Add the remaining milk and stir until well blended. Top with a dollop of whipped topping and sprinkles. Serve with a straw.

Warm Yoo-Hoo

Pour the milk into small saucepan and heat on low. Stir in chocolate syrup and cinnamon and cook until very warm but not boiling.

Serve in your favorite mug with whipped topping and sprinkles.

The University of Oregon opened in 1876. Five seniors received graduation diplomas in 1878. Today more than 22,000 students attend, giving plenty of opportunities to say Yoo-Hoo and meet someone new.

Placekicker
PRETZELS

Ingredients

32 flat weave-type pretzels

4 packs (32 individual
   candies) Rolos

32 raw brown almonds

Green sanding sugar

2 tablespoons
   powdered sugar

A splash of milk

✱ Serves 20–25 ✱

Preheat oven to 250 degrees. Cover a baking sheet with parchment paper.

Place pretzels on baking sheet 1 inch apart. Place 1 chocolate on top of each pretzel. Bake for 3 minutes; remove from oven immediately.

While still on the baking sheet, gently press one almond into each warm candy until sides come up slightly but do not cover almond. Immediately sprinkle with green sanding sugar.

In a small bowl, mix powdered sugar and milk into a semi-thick glaze, adding more sugar or milk as needed to get correct consistency. Using a toothpick, draw thin lines on top of almonds for a football look. Cool and serve.

Placekickers are part of the Special Teams unit. This is a special treat, and one that will feed lots of fans.

Beaver
TURNOVERS

Ingredients

1 frozen puff pastry sheet, thawed

Flour

3 tablespoons orange marmalade, divided

Powdered sugar

2 tablespoons miniature chocolate chips

$1/4$ teaspoon butter or margarine

$1/2$ teaspoon half-and-half, divided

Green and yellow nonpareils

✳ Serves 6 ✳

Preheat oven to 400 degrees. Spread a large sheet of parchment paper onto a flat surface and lightly sprinkle with flour. Unfold pastry and place on parchment paper.

Cut 6 (3-inch) squares along folds. Spoon $1/2$ tablespoon orange marmalade into the center of each square. Quickly fold squares into triangles, carefully keeping marmalade in center. Seal edges with a fork along sides.

Place turnovers on a baking sheet covered with parchment paper and bake 12–15 minutes or until golden brown. Remove from oven and let cool 10 minutes. Lightly dust tops with powdered sugar.

Place chocolate chips in a small microwave-safe bowl. Microwave on high 50–60 seconds, remove immediately, and stir vigorously until melted. Add butter and stir. Mix in $1/4$ teaspoon half-and-half and stir. Microwave for 10 seconds and stir again. Add remaining half-and-half, stir, and microwave for another 10 seconds. Drizzle chocolate sauce onto each turnover and sprinkle with nonpareils.

Beaver turnovers are always fun for Duck fans, this one is delicious, too.

Mighty Oregon®
GOLD BARS

Ingredients

1 box yellow cake mix

3 eggs, divided

1/2 cup melted butter

8 ounces cream cheese
(not low-fat)

1 teaspoon vanilla

1 pound confectioner's sugar

Green and yellow
sanding sugar

Makes 16–24 squares ✳

Preheat oven to 350 degrees. Grease a 9 x 12-inch baking pan.

In a large bowl, combine cake mix, 1 egg, and butter; press into the prepared pan.

In another large bowl, beat cream cheese, remaining eggs, vanilla, and sugar on medium speed until well mixed. Pour over the cake. Bake for 45 minutes or until golden brown.

Lightly sprinkle sanding sugars over the top. Cool 30 minutes and then chill for 1 hour before cutting into squares and serving in pan.

Oregon's gold rush peaked in 1858, but continues as the Ducks go for the gold, silver, and crystal BCS trophy.

Yell-O®
GELL-O BOWL CAKE

Ingredients

1 box angel food cake mix

1 small box lemon flavor
  instant pudding

1 pint heavy whipping cream

Yellow nonpareils

1 jar (6 ounces)
  green maraschino
  cherries, optional

* Serves 6–8 *

Bake cake according to directions on box, using any pan size, and cool for 1 hour. Remove cake from pan and cut into 2-inch pieces.

Place half of the pieces into a medium-size, round bowl. Mix pudding according to directions on box and pour half over cake in bowl. Add the rest of the cake then the remaining pudding. Using a spatula, spread pudding evening over the cake pieces and lightly compress them into place. Refrigerate overnight or 6 hours.

Using a knife, ease the cake away from the sides of the bowl and flip over onto a serving plate.

In a medium bowl, beat whipping cream on high until peaks form. Frost the cake with whipped cream, sprinkle with nonpareils, and decorate with maraschino cherries, if using.

The Ducks have been to the Rose Bowl, Cotton Bowl, Sun, Fiesta, and Holiday Bowls, the Aloha, Las Vegas, and Seattle Bowls, the Independence, Freedom, and Liberty Bowls, and the BCS Championship, which wasn't a bowl but was a whole lot of fun.

59

Pear-O-Ducks
COFFEE CAKE

Ingredients

3/4 cup shortening

3 eggs

1 3/4 cups flour

1 1/2 cups packed
   brown sugar

1/2 teaspoon baking powder

1/2 teaspoon baking soda

1/4 teaspoon nutmeg

1 1/4 teaspoons cinnamon

1 teaspoon vanilla

2 firm pears, chopped
   into 1/4-inch pieces

1/2 cup slivered almonds

✳ Serves 12 ✳

Preheat oven to 350 degrees. Prepare a Bundt or tube pan with nonstick cooking spray.

Beat all ingredients except pears and almonds in a large bowl until incorporated into a batter. Add pears and almonds, and beat for 1 minute on medium speed. Pour into prepared pan and level with a spatula. Bake for 40 minutes or until an inserted toothpick comes out clean. Let stand 5 minutes then flip cake onto a serving plate. Cool 1 hour and drizzle with Yell-O® and Big Green® Glaze.

About 9,000 acres of pears are grown in Oregon. Ducks do not eat pears, but Oregon Ducks® do as part of specialized diet plans through the U of O™ Sports Nutrition Program.

Yell-O® and Big Green® Glaze

1 cup confectioner's sugar

2¹/₂ teaspoons milk

3 drops yellow food coloring

3 to 5 drops green food coloring

In a small bowl, combine sugar and milk, adjusting the amount of sugar and milk as needed to get a drizzling consistency. Equally divide glaze between 2 small bowls. Tint 1 bowl of glaze yellow and the other green. Drizzle yellow glaze over cake and let harden. Cover bowl of green glaze with a dampened paper towel until ready to use. When yellow glaze has hardened, drizzle green glaze over the top.

Quack Attack™
FOOTBALL CAKE

Ingredients

1 box yellow cake mix

3 eggs

1 cup water

Green and yellow food color

**2 tubs (16 ounces each)
   vanilla frosting**

✳ Serves 10–14 ✳

Preheat oven to 350 degrees. Prepare football-shaped cake pan with nonstick cooking spray, leaving the top 2 inches uncoated.

In a large bowl, beat cake mix, eggs, and water on low for 1 minute. Increase speed and beat batter until visible lumps are gone. Batter will be very creamy. Drop 8 to 10 drops of green food color into the batter and gently swirl through with a knife. Do not mix; just leave the streaks of color. Pour batter into prepared pan.

Bake for 40 minutes or until an inserted toothpick comes out clean. Cool in pan 5 minutes then flip football out onto a cooling rack.

Tint 1 tub of frosting yellow and the other green. Frost the cake with the yellow and use the green frosting to decorate the football with strips, lacings, and the Oregon™ O. You can make "grass" on your serving plate by piping the frosting with a star tip on your pastry bag.

Excitement mounts as the Oregon Ducks® take the field and another thrilling hour of football begins! GO DUCKS!

C. J. GIFFORD is a freelance writer based in Portland, Oregon. She regularly attends UO™ football games where she honed her tailgating technique. When she's not cheering on the Ducks, she spends time in the kitchen and garden, traveling, and writing.